HISTORIA E NUMRAVE

THE NUMBER STORY

SMALL BOOK ONE

ENGLISH - ALBANIAN

Numbers Teach Children
Their Number Names

written and illustrated by

MISS ANNA

Early Reader Edition of *The Number Story 1*
Bronze Medal Winner, 2016 Wishing Shelf Book Award

Library of Congress Control Number: 2018902040

Names: Miss Anna, author.
Title: Number story : numbers teach children their number names / Miss Anna.
Description: Portland, OR: Lumpy Publishing, 2018.
Identifiers: ISBN 978-1-945977-51-0 | LCCN 2018902040
Summary: The pictures and rhymes present stories which introduce numbers 0-10.
Subjects: LCSH Numeration—English--Albanian--Pictorial works--Juvenile literature. | BISAC JUVENILE NONFICTION /
Languages: English--Albanian
Classification: LCC QA141.3 .M57 2018 | DDC 513—dc23

Publisher: Lumpy Publishing
Website: www.missannabooks.com
Email: missanna@missannabooks.com

Paperback: ISBN 978-1-945977-51-0
Printed in the U.S.A.   1 3 5 7 9 10 8 6 4 2

Ke dëshirë të mësosh

emrat e numrave?

It is very easy and a lot of fun!

Është shumë e thjeshtë

dhe shumë argëtuese!

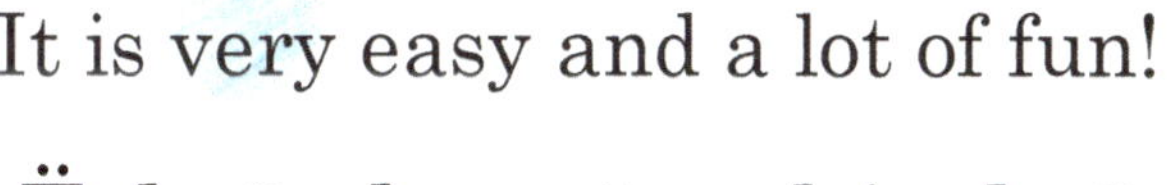

Say-along our little jingle

Ta recitojmë bashkē kētë vjershë të vogël!

starting from Number One!

Do ta nisim me Numrin Një!

1

ONE   looks like my one finger.

NJË

ngjan me një gisht.

ONE!
NJË!

2
TWO trails a tail.
DY
ka një bisht.

A TAIL! NJË BISHT!

3

THREE has bumps.

TRE

ka gunga.

BUMPY! ME GUNGA!

4
FOUR carries a sail.
KATËR
ka një velë anijeje.

4
A SAIL!
VELË
ANIJEJE!

5

FIVE   is a racing track.

PESË

është një pistë garash.

VROOM
VRUUUM!
1

6

SIX curves like a snail.

GJASHTË

mblidhet si kërmill.

A SNAIL! SI KËRMILL!

7

SEVEN has a sharp angle.

SHTATË

ka një kënd me majë.

OUCH!
OU!

8

EIGHT   is rollercoaster rails.

TETË

është si shina cirku.

URRA!
YIPPEE!

NINE   is a bubble on a stick.

NËNTË

eshtë një flluskë në shkop.

A BUBBLE! NJË FLLUSKË!

TEN   is an eye of a whale.

DHJETË

ështe si syri i një balene.

WINK!
SHKEL SYRIN!

And
Dhe
O
ZERO is an empty pail.
ZERO
është një kovë bosh.

IT'S EMPTY!
Është Bosh!

Thank you for playing with us today.

We had a lot of fun too!

Faleminderit që luajtet me ne sot.

U argëtuam shumë edhe ne!

We are your Number friends,
Zero to Ten,
Who will be here for you~
Ne jemi Numrat, miqtë e tu
Nga Zero në Dhjetë.
Për ty këtu do të jemi gjithmonë.

Bye-bye now!
See you again soon!
Pafshim!
Do shihemi prapë
shumë shpejt!

The Numbers are *SINGING* too!

To sing-a-long, look for Miss Anna Number Story
at your favorite music store like iTUNES.

MP3

Numbers 0-10
IDENTIFYING
& COUNTING

Numbers 11-20
& Ordinals

first, second, third...

Numbers 0-100
& Place Values

ones, tens, hundreds...

About Clock
& Telling Tim

hours, minutes, secon

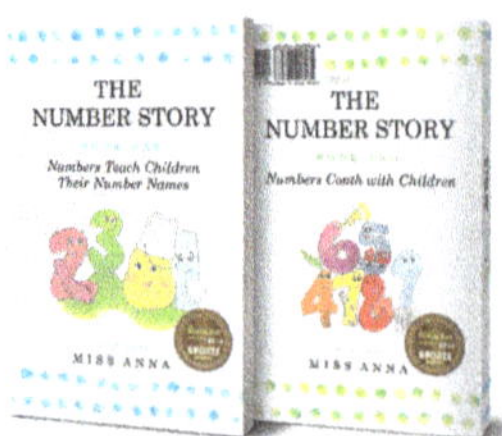

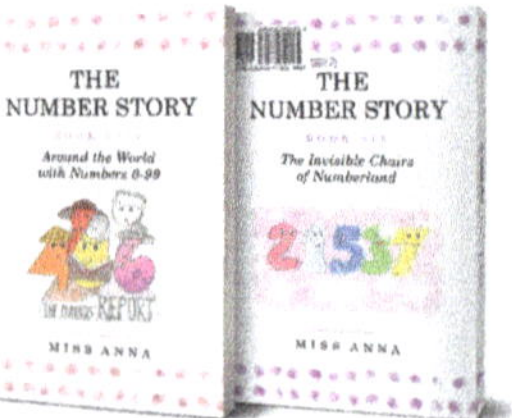

Number Story 1 & 2

isbn: 978-0-996216-48-7

Number Story 3 & 4

isbn: 978-1-945977-01-5

Number Story 5 & 6

isbn: 978-1-945977-06-0

Number Story 7 &

isbn: 978-1-949320-40

For more Miss Anna books to love,
visit us at

w w w . m i s s a n n a b o o k s . c o m

Numbers are working hard all over the world!
Come Travel the World with Us!